To:

From:

Be Your Own Boss

How to Start or Buy a Business

Anthony Zaffuto

Copyright 2023
Anthony Zaffuto

Be Your Own Boss
How to Start or Buy a Business

All Rights Reserved

No text or images in this book may be used
or reproduced in any manner without
written permission of Anthony Zaffuto.

This publication is designed to provide accurate
and authoritative information. Neither the author
nor publisher is engaged in providing legal,
accounting, or other professional service.

All brand names and product names listed in this book are trademarks,
registered trademarks or trade names of their respective holders.

Photo Credits:
All images from iStock by Getty Images, istockphoto.com.
Credits for images on the following pages:
2, anyaberkat; 10, relif; 14, andresr; 18, fizkes; 22, airdone; 26, AnnaFrajtova; 28, aldomurillo; 30, Marcus Clackson; 38, andresr; 40, IvelinRadkov; 42, Peshkova; 46, kupicoo; 50, jacoblund; 56, vasabil; 60, mapodile; 64, nd3000; 68, sturti; 70, miniseries; 74, laflor; 78, AndreyPopov; 82, Ridofranz; 84, Jacob Wackerhausen; 88, AndreyPopov; 92, sturti; 100, atakan.

ISBN: 978-1-7375505-8-7

Cover Layout and Interior Layout: Capri Porter
Edited by BizSuccessBooks.com

Published by
Legacies & Memories, LLC, St. Augustine, Florida
BizSuccessBooks.com
LegaciesandMemoriesPublishing.com

Purchase This Book Online
amazon.com · BarnesandNoble.com · Bookshop.org · Other Retailers

To Purchase Large Quantities
Contact us for Special Corporate Discounts
(888) 862-2754 or BizSuccessBooks.com

Dedication

This is dedicated to the one I love: Sharon Ann Monaghan Zaffuto, my college sweetheart who I married as soon as possible after we graduated.

To our children:
Danny and his wife Sandra and their children: Sunny, Murphy, Blair (and Blair's children Gavin and Mason), Justin, and Hannah.

Margie and her daughter Dakota.

Anthony and his wife Andrea and their children: Roman, Ava, and Mia.

"Believe you can and you are halfway there."

Theodore Roosevelt

Contents

Dedication
Introduction

PART I: STARTING A BUSINESS

Find a Job You Love and You Will Never Work a Day in Your Life	15
Prepare a Personal SWOT Analysis: Identify Your Strengths, Weaknesses, Opportunities and Threats	19
Find a Market Niche – a Small Section of a Larger Market	23
Map Your Market	27
Sell People What THEY Want to Buy – Not What YOU Want to Sell Them	29
Demonstrate a Sustainable Distinctive Advantage Over Competitors	31

    Quality
    Service
    Price
    Location and Leasing
    Common Area Maintenance (CAM)
    Office
    The 10 Percent Rule

Learn to Be a Proficient Planner	39
Create Your Own Brand	41

Marketing   43
    Review Your Own Website
    Phone Calls
    Products
    Conduct Research
    Become a Super Salesperson   47

Surround Yourself with Terrific People   51

Follow the Golden Rule   55

Cash is King   57

Prepare a SWOT Analysis on a New Business   61

Have Fun – and Don't Take Yourself Too Seriously   65

PART II: BUYING A BUSINESS

Buying an Existing Business   69

Ask Questions   69

Major Advantages of Buying an Existing Business   71
    Financial History
    Financing
    Bank Relationship
    Suppliers
    Assets
    Inventory
    Training

Buyer's Leverage   75

Prepare a SWOT Analysis When Purchasing an Existing Business	79
Seller's Expectation	83

What the Purchase Price Usually Includes
    Current Market Value of Physical Assets
    Projected Income Stream
	85

Agreeing on a Selling Price Goodwill	89

Why Existing Businesses (and New Ones) Fail
    Under-Capitalized
    Poor Planning
    Poor Management
    Bad Location
	93

Investing in a Franchise	101
About the Author	105
From the Publisher...	107

Introduction

So, you have always wanted to be your own boss – or at least you dreamed about not having to work for anyone. Why have you not pursued the idea?

Fear? Too complicated? Not sure you have what it takes to be on your own? Don't have financing? Or maybe you just can't figure out how to make the transition from working for someone to becoming a business owner.

It is not easy, but it is possible.

Ask almost any entrepreneur or owner and they will likely tell you it's great running their own show. But it's not without headaches. It's not for the faint-hearted. You must be all-in and resilient if you are to be successful.

From determining whether you are suited to being an owner to figuring out what type of business and where it should be located, you will find expert advice in this book. It's chockfull of practical information and loaded with questions you can ask yourself – all aimed at providing important details about the many aspects of ownership.

Part I focuses on Starting a Business. **An entrepreneur is someone who takes risks by starting a business.**

Let's be clear, becoming an entrepreneur is the hardest and least successful way to ownership, and it usually takes the longest time to reach profitability, if ever. It has the highest fatality rate. Expect a constant process of overcoming challenges. Despite the hard work to get the concept off the ground, there is no guarantee the doors will ever open or that you will generate the level of revenue to be profitable.

On the flip side, the rewards of being a successful entrepreneur can be life changing. That includes having more freedom, being your own boss, becoming financially independent, and building an asset that could be expanded and sold.

Part II focuses on Buying a Business. The quickest way to becoming a successful owner is to acquire an established and successful firm. Products and services can be sampled, financial records can be examined, and staff can be reviewed. The prospective owner should spend time with the seller and learn what has worked and not worked – and why. Inquire as to what could be done to enhance the company. When negotiations and the closing are finalized, the new owner benefits instantly from an income stream.

Part II also features another way of buying: franchising. Becoming a franchisee carries many advantages that are not usually part of buying an independently owned business. Franchisors have a history of running successful companies and when you buy into their concept and operating model, you will have the benefit of their expertise. Plus, they will guide you because your success is their success.

One major downside: there is often a hefty price for becoming a franchisee. You also won't have the kind of independence or freedom you would have otherwise. Examine the list of the many pluses and minuses of investing in a franchise to determine if it's right for you.

"Too often, entrepreneurs are forgotten heroes. We rarely hear about them. But look into the heart of America, and you'll see them. They're the owners of that store down the street, the faithful who support our churches, schools, and communities, the brave people everywhere who produce our goods, feed a hungry world, and keep our homes and families warm while they invest in the future to build a better America."

Ronald Reagan

PART I

Find a Job You Love and You Will Never Work a Day in Your Life

This nugget of wisdom has been around a long time, perhaps even spoken by Confucius, one of the wisest of men. He and others who believed it must have known the difficulty of hard work because they urged people to direct their energies into something that would be fun to do. Clearly, this principle is true in starting a business.

Rule number one: It must be something that you love to do because when you face inevitable problems, they will wear you down unless you love your work.

Also, remember that your venture better be fun because when you work for yourself, you will be working for the toughest boss you have ever had: Yourself.

Never be afraid to try something new. Remember, amateurs built the ark; professionals built the Titanic.

Before starting out, list your reasons for wanting to go into business. Some of the most common reasons:
- To be your own boss
- To have creative freedom
- To become financially independent
- To fully use your skills and knowledge
- You have something in common with successful entrepreneurs. You left jobs due to differences with those above you. This is a common trait of self-directed people. You would love to run your own show.

- You admire a certain company for its products and services. It happens to be for sale.
- A firm offers franchises and you are aware of an underserved area with little or no competition. You would eagerly enter the franchisor's training program and would enjoy selling their products and services.

Ask yourself these questions to determine what business is right for you:

- What do others say I am good at?
- What do I like to do with my time?
- What technical skills have I learned or developed?
- Do I have any hobbies or interests that are marketable?
- How much time do I have to run a successful business?
- Do I have sufficient resources to invest in a particular business including cash, borrowing power and physical needs the venture might require?
- Having the right people is crucial. Have I discussed the opportunity with others, particularly those who I might want to have on board as either an employee or co-investor?

"When work is a pleasure, life is joy! When work is a duty, life is slavery."

Maxim Gorky

Prepare a Personal SWOT Analysis: Identify Your Strengths, Weaknesses, Opportunities and Threats

Strengths
- Willing to take risks
- Enjoy working with people
- Blessed with a high energy level
- Self-starter generally needing little direction
- Willing to work long hours especially during startup
- Several years of experience in retail and service businesses
- Love the nature of the venture such as sports, music, food preparation, etc.
- From savings, have money to invest at least to cover a down payment, and have borrowing ability
- Family and friends interested in the idea have mentioned the possibility of becoming co-investors.

Weaknesses
- Enjoy good but not great credit
- Don't really like dealing with the public
- Limited amount of cash to put into the business
- No experience dealing with the core products being sold
- No experience locating or dealing with suppliers of this industry
- Borrowing would mean a second mortgage or a home equity loan.
- Because of an old injury, cannot lift heavy merchandise or equipment.
- Do not like paperwork. Would need help with bookkeeping, payroll, bill paying, and correspondence.
- Have been known to lose my temper when dealing with difficult people and those not willing to work as hard as I do.

Opportunities
- The area is among the fastest growing in the state.
- My spouse has expressed a willingness to take a course in accounting to help with the bookkeeping.
- A local college has a three-hour, one night a week course in Entrepreneurship/Small Business Management I could take.

Threats
- It could be difficult and expensive to find and attract staff with desirable experience.
- Problems with my long-term injury could become worse, lessening my ability to be on the sales floor, standing, lifting, moving inventory, and stocking shelves.
- We have savings in part due to my spouse's income as a critical care nurse. If he or she enters the business to help with office work, that income will be lost.
- We are a couple approaching the age of 30 with no children. As desirable as having a child or children is, it would not be helpful for the business.

"I've failed over and over again in my life and that is why I succeed."

Michael Jordan

Find a Market Niche – a Small Section of a Larger Market

Why go head-to-head with the big fellows?

When Steve Jobs and Steve Wozniak created their first Apple computer, IBM controlled more than 75 percent of the computer industry. IBM was so dominant that the U.S. Justice Department filed a lawsuit in federal court accusing the company of being a monopoly. At the time, other competitors were GE, RCA, Honeywell, and other billion-dollar companies.

Rather than challenge the giants in large computers, the two Steves sought a small niche in the market for the personal computer. The features it offered and the problems it solved had been ignored by the big players who thought the personal computer was too small to deal with.

Similarly, you – as a new entrepreneur – should be pursuing a niche strategy and looking for a specific aspect of a larger market that the giants are ignoring or underserving.

Generally, there are two successful reasons to enter a market:

1. The area is currently not served with your intended product or service.
2. The area has suppliers, but they are not doing a good job.

Identify the niche your business will fill. Ask yourself the following questions:
- Who is my competition?
- Can I deliver a higher-quality service?

- Can I create a demand for my business?
- Is my idea practical and will it fill a need?
- What are my business advantages over existing firms?

"There is no such thing as success in a bad business."

Elbert Hubbard

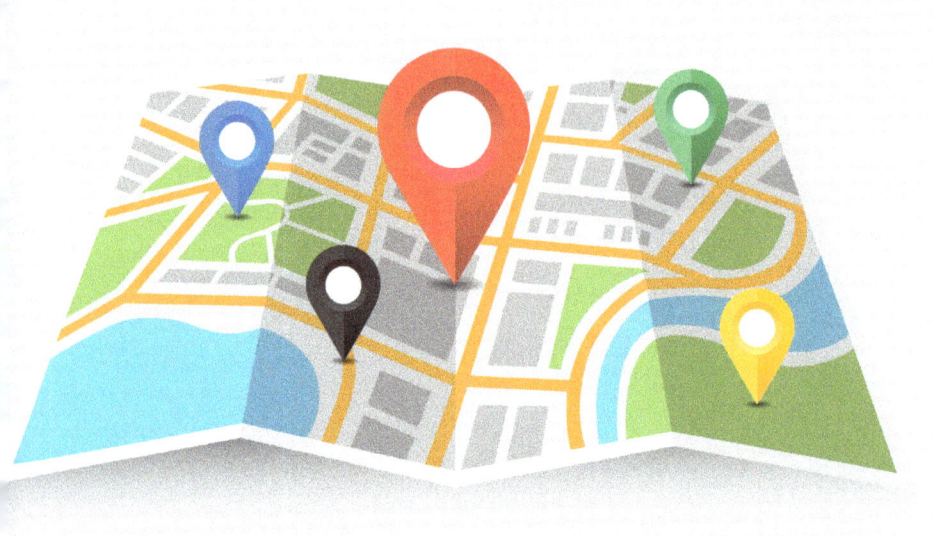

Map Your Market

On a map, locate existing competitors. For example, opening a new or acquiring an existing Mexican restaurant is under consideration. Create a code for use on the map. Existing Mexican restaurants are pinpointed with the codes A1, A2, A3, etc.

The strongest competitor is labeled A1, the next serious competitor A2, etc. Secondary competitors are identified such as non-Mexican restaurants carrying tacos and/or nachos. They are labeled B1, B2, etc.

Suppose the business under consideration is in hardware. The locations of Home Depot and Lowe's would be designated with the "A" category because they have broad and deep inventory. Direct competitors such as Ace Hardware would be the "B" category. Indirect competitors such as Wal-Mart and Target would be "C" competitors because they, too, carry a small line of hardware.

Consider how wide the map should be. How far would you drive to a Mexican restaurant or a Home Depot?

When you have finished with the map, the conclusion might be the market is saturated. Even so, this will have been a worthwhile exercise if it stops you from launching an unsuccessful venture.

Sell People What THEY Want to Buy – Not What YOU Want to Sell Them

Ask anyone: "Does McDonald's make the best hamburger?" Chances are, the response will be, "No."

Why, then, does McDonald's have more than 14,000 restaurants in the United States. And why are the average annual sales between $2.7 million and $4 million?

The reason is because McDonald's sells what people want to buy, not necessarily what the company would like to sell. Americans still want hamburgers, but clearly, they have told the company they want other products that are not fried, not red meat, are better for them and are still inexpensive.

In your search for a market niche, find products or services that people want, but are not getting to their satisfaction.

How do you find out about potential niches? You conduct the most basic and least expensive form of market research: Ask potential customers and your family and friends about their wants and needs – and whether those are being met satisfactorily.

Every successful business either satisfies a want or a need in a market. If your business concept will not do so, why should it exist?

Gain some experience in your chosen field before you begin your own business because that will help you understand what the customer wants. Don't assume you know what customers want. Ask them!

Demonstrate a Sustainable Distinctive Advantage Over Competitors

Your business should have a sustainable distinguishing feature or an extraordinary difference that provides an advantage over your competitors. Generally, the possibilities fall in one of these categories:
- Quality
- Service
- Price
- Location

Build your business on at least one of these four cornerstones. And notice the order in which they appear.

Quality
It means meeting or exceeding customer expectations. It takes a greater effort to produce superb quality or fantastic service. But then you will have something sustainable and proprietary, which your competitors cannot easily match.

When you think of a business based on quality, think of Disney World. The theme park focuses on delivering an experience unmatched by other attractions. Accordingly, Disney can charge high prices and customers are willing to endure long lines.

Chick-fil-A averages about $8 million in annual sales per location – at least double that of McDonald's! What is their quality advantage? They sell chicken and everyone knows it is healthier than consuming red meat – and it's lower in calories. Another quality advantage may be the fact they downplay the issue of "fried" compared to KFC restaurants. Chick-fil-A also seems to provide better service. That's evident, in part, because of the training they provide for their workers.

Service

Let's say you notice the local Italian restaurant does not deliver. This appears to be an opportunity to start a low-cost business that only delivers. Fortunately, the costs and risks will be limited because only a small facility in a low-rent area will be needed.

Your new business opens with a competitive advantage – it delivers. A marketing program announces home delivery is now available, and the delivery-only firm initially is kept busy with orders.

- How long will it take for the existing Italian restaurant to notice its revenue is shrinking?
- How long will it take for that restaurant to figure out what is causing its customer count and takeout orders to shrink?
- How long will it take for that restaurant to offer home delivery even though it was considered when the business started, but not offered because of the headaches involved?

The point is, after the Italian restaurant is forced to offer home delivery, will your competing new delivery-only service have a sustainable competitive advantage? No, it will be neutralized. Its survival will now rest on quality, price, or location.

For companies built on service and convenience, think of an automated carwash or an oil change operation that guarantees quick service.

Price

For businesses built on price, consider Wal-Mart and its Sam's Warehouse stores. Notice that only the well-established giants can have price as their only competitive advantage. Consider Amazon, another giant that competes on price, but also service with its promise of quick delivery.

Having the lowest price is the weakest distinctive advantage. A competitor selling the same product or delivering the same service can always undercut you, especially if it decides to discontinue a product line or has an inventory reduction sale. A competitor with deep pockets could initiate a price war knowing it can drive the smaller firm out of existence.

Location and Leasing

Where your business is located can be a sustainable competitive advantage at times, even when it may not offer the highest quality or best service. Of course, study the area and consider what changes might be coming. A competitor could be moving into the area.

When leasing a space for your new firm, know that it is not always simple. Factors include how the lease is structured to whether your annual rent may be tied to the volume of your sales.

Rent in General: Obviously, the larger the area being leased, the higher the rent. In most cases it is negotiable based on supply and demand. Thus, two stores of the same size next door to one another can be paying different amounts. If this is a highly desirable shopping center and a spot becomes available, the landlord will try to charge a premium. Conversely, some centers are on a decline. If many spaces are open, the tenant should be able to negotiate a discount.

Rent in Malls: In the nation's highly desirable enclosed malls, the landlord generally negotiates to receive the higher of two figures:

- The negotiated annual rent. Assume it is $96,000 annually which is paid in 12 monthly installments of $8,000.
- A negotiated percentage of sales. The prospective tenant must provide an annual sales forecast. If it is too low, the landlord does not want the firm in the mall. Assume the prospective tenant provides an annual sales forecast of $1,000,000. Assume the landlord insists the rent will be 10 percent of sales. This would amount to $100,000. At the end of Year 1, the tenant so far will have paid $96,000 in rent.

    Now assume the final sales figure happens to agree with the forecast of $1,000,000. Ten percent of that number is $100,000 compared to the $96,000 paid. The tenant must make up the difference by paying $4,000 more in rent.

    Suppose the actual sales figure is only $900,000. Ten percent would amount to $90,000. Nothing more would be owed.

Why does the landlord gain such a sizable advantage, receiving an expensive monthly rent or even more if the tenant enjoys a high sales year? His argument is, if your store enjoys a high-volume year, it is due in part to the strength of the mall and therefore he should benefit. The nation's most desirable enclosed malls have a waiting list. The landlord knows how many leases are coming to an end. He has the intention of raising renewal terms to drive out less than high-volume stores. Not surprisingly, he will try to maximize rental income.

Common Area Maintenance (CAM): Shopping areas are expensive to maintain. Costs cover the entrance, buildings, signage, landscaping, garbage removal, security, insurance, and property taxes. Additionally, the major expenditure is often the parking lot, including paving, resealing, painting parking stripes and directional arrows. Add snow removal in many parts of the country. Landlords pass on the costs to the tenants, usually proportionately. A store with 2,000 square feet of the center's 200,000 square feet has one percent of the leased area and will generally pay one percent of the common area maintenance costs.

Enclosed malls have additional expenses, including the cost of running an office, supplying and cleaning restrooms, and the maintenance of aisle floors, sprinklers, and audio systems. In addition, tenants are usually required to share in marketing and advertising costs, including staging promotional events. Now consider the most expensive overhead item: heating and air conditioning the thousands of cubic square feet under the roof. Because all overhead items are passed on proportionally to the tenants, in some cases CAM could be as much as the rent. It would include you paying the landlord's insurance and property taxes, both of which are part of what is known as a triple net lease.

Office: If you open the type of business that allows you to work from home – and local zoning laws allow it – you obviously save money. But weigh the advantages and disadvantages of working at home, especially from your clients' viewpoints. Will they consider you or your firm less professional if you don't have an office? If you need to meet clients in person, can you rent a meeting room or conference room somewhere?

Let's say you are an engineer, architect, or software developer, or you have another type of service business where having an office outside your home is not necessary. Then you might consider a virtual office – a legally recognized location that allows you to use it as your firm's official address where your mail is delivered and where your occupational or business license can be posted. Some virtual offices offer telephone answering services and access to conference rooms. A virtual office is generally less to rent than a private office. If a shared workspace is what you prefer or need, it also can cost less than a private office.

If you do lease a private office, know that many landlords require you to have liability insurance to cover accidents or other mishaps on their property. This will be an expense above the monthly rent. Also, as is the case with leasing a space for a store, you may have CAM expenses, depending on the landlord and the office building.

The 10 Percent Rule: Annual Occupancy Expense (Rent + CAM) should not exceed 10 percent of Annual Revenue. Businesses incur major expenses for payroll, the cost of goods sold, and overhead. When occupancy expense is greater than 10 percent of Annual Revenue, the business owner is working for the landlord, not himself. The exception is when payroll, cost of goods sold, or overhead items are small. Examples would include one-person firms or a business operating out of a home.

> "If you don't speculate, you can't accumulate."
>
> **English Proverb**

Learn to Be a Proficient Planner

Chance favors the prepared mind. If you fail to plan, then you are planning to fail. What is the use of running if you are running on the wrong side of the road?

Let's face it. Most people are not good at planning for a firm because they have not developed the skill it takes to put together a business plan. You may be skilled at scheduling and arranging timetables, which are short-term techniques. But a plan includes a mission statement, a description of the business, a marketing strategy, financial statement projections, and other fairly sophisticated techniques. If you are like most folks, you will need help developing your business plan.

Potential partners and lenders generally require this written plan outlining the long-term objectives. Even more important, the strategies and tactics that will accomplish the objectives must be spelled out.

In short, you must have a vision of what your business can become – and a game plan for achieving that vision.

Success comes from having the proper aim, as well as the right ammunition.

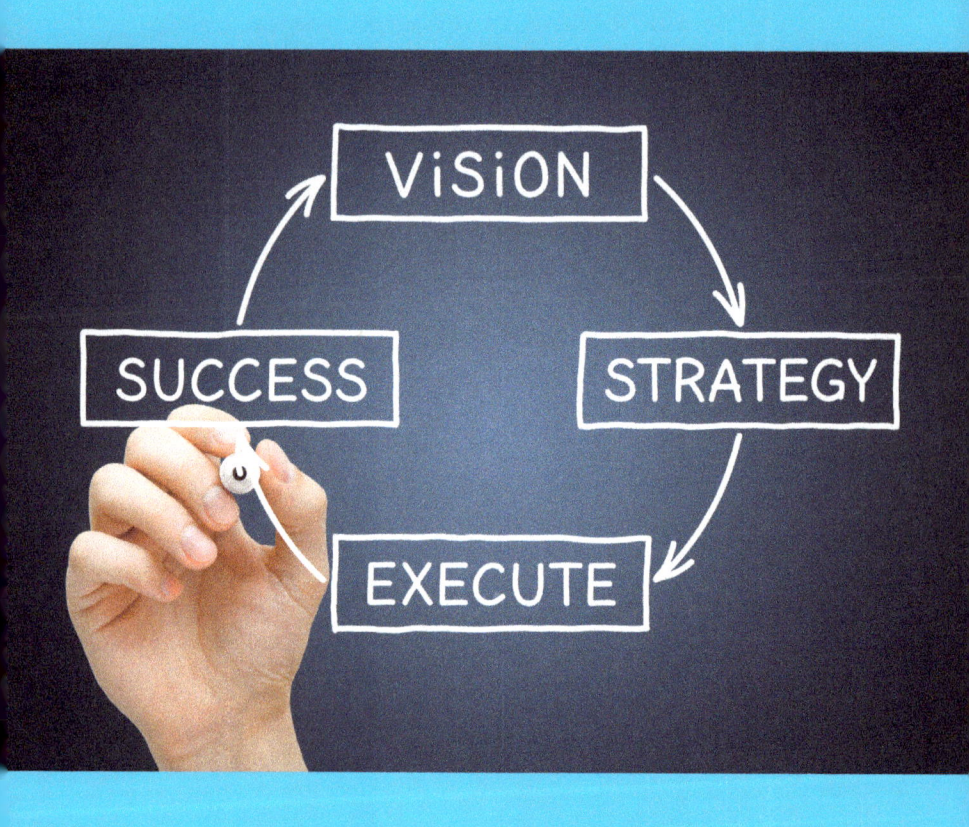

Create Your Own Brand

Creating your own brand means creating your own identity. Think of the genius and uniqueness in the names, Google and Starbucks.

Begin by defining: Who is your primary targeted audience? Is it male or primarily female? Young crowd or old? Upper income or lower? The point is, you cannot be all things to all people. Have one strong demographic image of your ideal customer. Play to that person first by identifying his or her needs. The Greeks coined the word, demographic, to mean "a picture of the people" they had in mind.

A fellow by the name of Herbert Swope once said, "I cannot give you a formula for success. But I can give you the formula for failure: try to please everybody."

Next, consider positioning: the way you wish the public to view your firm. If you desire potential customers to think of your business as providing superb quality, then create the right physical environment.

Think of an uncommon name that describes what your company is or does. Create or have a professional design a classy logo. Select a distinctive print style and have this unique identity appear on everything the public sees – signs, business cards, stationery, advertising, and any place your firm or its name are featured.

Through repeated usage, your brand identity will become familiar to people – and they will become comfortable with your business.

Marketing

How will you market your concept? Most new businesses, and many existing ones, must be able to get the word out about their services or products.

When you start, it's not enough to have expertise or even a service or product someone wants or needs. You must find ways to attract customers or clients. You could be the world's greatest plumber or electrician, or chiropractor, or computer whiz, or video game designer, but if no one knows you exist, then you won't be in business for long. Perhaps you create an online store or another internet-based enterprise. You still need marketing.

Marketing possibilities are endless, including digital and print advertising, websites, search engine optimization, e-mail, social media presence, social media advertising, newsletters, blogs, podcasts, direct mail, sponsorships, alliances with other businesses, public relations, earned media (news stories), radio, television, and much, much more.

The type of marketing and the strategies and tactics you employ will depend on the type of business or service you have. But all marketing should be aimed at reaching a specific audience. If an owner says his or her customer is anyone or everyone, then he or she doesn't know their primary customer. Identify your ideal customer or client by age, gender, income, interests, shopping habits and other characteristics. Only then can you start to determine where they are and how to reach them.

It is also important to know your competitors and the type of customers they have. You will then know what differentiates your company from theirs.

You can enhance your marketing by understanding customer service and the level of service you want to provide. For many companies, their customer service is awful. Most would agree that it has gone downhill over the years. There are a few ways you can discover what customers want, simply by being a customer or potential customer.

- Review your own website. Is it easy to use? Does it engage the viewer? What is its purpose – to simply provide information like an online brochure or is it designed for potential customers to contact you? What is their incentive for giving their name and contacting you through the website?

  Know your customer. Be aware of any technical terms and issues that might frustrate non-technical users or older customers who find the website challenging to navigate.

  Some proprietors choose to not have a website. This is a major mistake. Potential customers want information, and they often want to find it easily without having to engage with anyone.

  Other business owners decide to have only a Facebook page instead of a website. But this, too, is less effective. An owner has far less control of his or her own fate because Facebook may suddenly change its rules or algorithms. The owner has little choice as to how their page looks and maybe even the type of information that can be displayed.

- Phone calls. Does it take too long for someone to answer when a potential customer calls? As a customer, have you noticed when you call, you are given several options, but none are what you are calling about?

If there's a recording, should there be? Or should you have a real person answer all calls? Even if you can't afford to hire someone, it's likely you can afford one of the many phone answering services if it's important that a caller doesn't reach a recording. If you have a recording, are the instructions easy to navigate or is it frustrating to use, leaving the customer with a bad impression, or worse, deciding to go elsewhere?

- Products. Have you as the owner or family members regularly used your products or services, or assembled the products to determine just how easy or difficult it is? Have you bought and assembled some of the products your competitors sell so you know the differences? Have you tasted the food your competitors sell? Or have you or people you know used some of your competitors' services?

- Conduct research. Visit the websites of companies in your industry. Make phone calls to see how inquiries are handled. Visit your competitors' stores. Ask family members and friends to visit and tell you their impressions. Have your employees do the same.

Become a Super Salesperson

Successful business owners must become super salespersons. After all, if they truly do not believe they have a fine product or service, who will? Why would customers leave your competitors to buy from you?

Owners discover that selling becomes easier the harder they work at it. And, the objective of a salesperson is not to make sales, but to make customers. How? By discovering through questions and research the unfilled needs and wants of customers. Don't rely on a "gut feel" or a "hunch."

The first thing a super salesperson does is to make a friend. A woman enters the store with a little girl. The salesperson remarks, "What a pretty sweetheart." Now, where do pretty little girls come from? Pretty women. The salesperson compliments the potential customer indirectly.

Although competition has grown fierce in every industry, in one sense becoming a super salesperson has gotten easier. The reason is that many families have two incomes and are more willing than ever to pay for two things they lack: Time and Convenience. Even single-person households or families with one income will purchase goods and services that save time or make their work easier. Think of the microwave, drive-through services, and the ever-increasing trend of home delivery by retailers such as Amazon, restaurants, supermarkets, pharmacies and others.

Also remember, it takes less effort to keep customers satisfied than to find new ones. You gained the business of regulars by solving their problems. But that does not mean you solved their problems forever. Thus, you must stay close to continue to be of help. When you fail to do that, you have lost them. Actually, customers are never really lost. Your competitor will find them.

A super salesperson is a problem-solver. That is why so many firms reward customers with exclusive discounts and loyalty programs.

"Everyone lives by selling something."

Robert Louis Stevenson

Surround Yourself with Terrific People

Even if you intend to design a firm with you as the only employee, help will be needed. Seeking the help of others is a strength, not a weakness. One hand cannot applaud. No one person knows everything that is needed to operate a successful business. A common error among many new owners is the belief that they suddenly have a monopoly on wisdom now that they are running their own show. Put another way, a person remains wise as long as they seek wisdom. The minute they think they have found all of it, they become a fool. What you learn after you think you know it all is what is most important.

There is an old Chinese saying, "Behind an able man, there are always other able men."

Customers, suppliers, creditors, and others will judge you by the people you surround yourself with, in and out of the firm.

Seek only high-quality people. If necessary, pay a little more for those who will represent you. There are many organizations that "hire on the cheap" because they think they cannot afford to pay more. But bad employees or service providers can generate badwill, which is the opposite of goodwill your marketing expenditures are trying to build.

Studies show passionate, high-quality staff members do not contribute 5 percent, 10 percent or even 20 percent more productivity. They generate greater than 100 percent more positive results than less motivated counterparts.

Accordingly, consider rewarding terrific folks with "a fraction of the action." Extra effort is reflected in bottom line profitability from both revenue and cost savings. For example, workers who benefit from profit sharing will turn off lights and equipment when not in use. When a customer asks, "Where can I find . . . ," motivated help will not just provide the aisle number. They will stop what they are doing and take the customer to the exact spot where product is located. If the product is missing or the customer has an additional question, the employee will refer to his cell phone to see the inventory status or will call a colleague.

Publix is by far the leading supermarket chain throughout the South. It tends to have highly motivated, customer-friendly staff. Why? It is a "closed" or "closely held corporation." Only employees and members of the board of directors can purchase shares of stock. By owning shares, employees are owners of the business. Like most corporations, increased profitability is reflected in dividend income and a rising value in the price of the stock.

Intelligent business owners know management is the art and science of getting things done through people.

"Success comes when people act together; failure tends to happen alone."

Deepak Chopra

"Character is what we are; reputation is what others think we are."

American Proverb

Follow the Golden Rule

"Do unto others as you would have them do unto you." This well-known piece of advice is centuries old. In fact, it predates Jesus by about 500 years.

Decide from day one that your business will follow the Golden Rule. Treat your customers, employees, suppliers, and even your competitors fairly. Treat them the way you would want to be treated.

James Cash (J.C.) Penney named his first venture The Golden Rule Stores to reflect his philosophy.

At the end of the day, you will have worked hard and deserve a good night's sleep. So, think of the good feeling you will have because you dealt with everyone in an honest manner. And remember, a half-truth is a whole lie.

Some think they have made a success of life when all they have made is a lot of money. The person who fails while trying to do good has more honor than the person who succeeds by taking advantage of others.

Integrity and wisdom are also an important part of the equation. Integrity means that when you promise a customer something, you keep that promise even if it means losing money on that transaction. Wisdom means not making such promises!

So, do unto others as though you were others.

Cash is King

If you ever forget that cash is king, all is lost. You are in business to maximize your cash! Not sales, not even profit, because profit in the accounting sense is not necessarily the same as cash. Accountants have clever ways of recording profit. But the only way of paying bills is to have cash.

You have probably played board games such as Monopoly. What happens if you own Boardwalk and Park Place, the two most valuable assets, yet you run out of cash because you keep landing on cheaper property? You lose! Many businesses have had millions invested in assets – land, buildings, equipment, inventory, etc. – but could not raise enough cash to pay accumulated debts. And it is very hard to liquidate those types of assets when you are desperate for cash. The result: bankruptcy, which is a fancy way of saying Lack of Cash.

When estimating startup capital for a leased site, remember that the landlord starts to collect rent the moment the key is turned over to the new tenant. It could take a month or two to fix up the space. For example, restaurants in a leased space typically require four months to build because refrigeration units must be installed, and plumbing and electrical systems must be updated. All during the building time, rent expense is incurred even though no sales are being recorded.

There is another common error in cash planning: "If I have enough cash to get the doors open, the new business should generate revenue to carry me through the first year." More often than not, establishing a customer base occurs more slowly than anticipated. But monthly expenses must be paid. An entrepreneur should anticipate and be prepared to possibly infuse a second round of investment sometime during the first year.

A related misconception is, "The venture should break even no later than the end of the first year." Once again, a start-up could require more than a year to become profitable and the owner must have access to additional operating funds. How long can the owner continue? Money is only lent to companies that have posted a positive cash flow for several years.

NEVER UNDERESTIMATE THE POWER OF CASH.

Georgia-Pacific Corp.

Sole text on one page of a two-page ad in Forbes magazine, July 23, 1990.

Prepare a SWOT Analysis on a New Business

Strengths
- Starting fresh you get to choose everything: Name, location, staff, inventory, equipment, etc.
  The converse is also true – you do not inherit anything old or bad.
- You can select a product or service that is currently hot and still early in the industry's life cycle.
  Doing so avoids competing in an industry passing through the maturity or decline stage.
- After researching the pluses and minuses of profitable industries, the most promising one that compliments your interests is chosen.
- Preparing a business plan maps out where you and the venture are, where you would like to take it, and how you plan to get there.
- Others can review the business plan and offer vital suggestions.

Weaknesses
- During startup no income will be earned, yet bills will be incurred.
- Starting from scratch, the venture must be built piece by piece, customer by customer. This will be a time-consuming process and mistakes are likely to be made.
- After several months of hard work and likely delays, the enterprise may never get off the ground.
  Time and money were invested, yet there may be nothing to show for the effort.

Opportunities
- The business plan outlines long-term goals and a road map of where the venture is headed. It should also highlight opportunities for expansion including potential new products and services,
  additional locations, and future partners through merger or acquisition.

Threats
- By the time the concept opens:
  o The cost of most things might rise more than budgeted.
  o Often the needed investment package has increased significantly due to unforeseen reasons.
  o The market and competitive environment could have changed and be a major cause of concern.
  o Negotiations with a landlord, construction firm, suppliers, and employees have become longer and tougher than anticipated.

"The longest journey begins with a single step."

20th Century Saying

Have Fun – and Don't Take Yourself Too Seriously

Enjoy! Starting a business appears easy to do, but developing a successful one is not. Once again, working for the most demanding of bosses – yourself – forces you to be thinking of your company every day and night.

In surveys of both successful and unsuccessful enterprises, the fundamental question asked was: "What has been the key that brought you fame or failure?" The reply most often was: "Hard work."

Prosperous companies tended to outwork the competition, especially during rough times. Failed business owners stated that although they worked hard, they were no longer prepared to put in the additional hard work – and additional savings – it would take to turn around their losing venture. So, they called it "quits."

Someone once said the mechanics of running a business are not really very complicated when you get down to the essentials. You must make some stuff and sell it for more than it costs you. That's about all there is to it except for a few million details. And those details require hard work if you are to be successful.

Successful folks battle the same odds as those who fail. But the winners have courage and believe in themselves. Courage does not mean avoiding risk, it means conquering it.

Achievers recognize that opportunity is the difference between success and failure. The trouble with opportunity is it comes disguised as hard work. And even when opportunity knocks, you still have to get up and open the door.

Winners take a plunge in starting their own business because worse than a quitter is the person who is afraid to begin.

"The greatest pleasure in life is doing what people say you cannot do."

Walter Bagehot, Prospective Review 1853 "Shakespeare."

PART II

Buying an Existing Business

Clearly, the easiest and quickest way to own a business is to buy one. It is also the safest way. Why? The primary reason: Time is money. In a very short time, an existing firm can be analyzed, and a decision can be reached: Is this a desirable firm to own?

Ask Questions

The first question generally is: Why is the business for sale? If it is doing well, why is the owner trying to unload it? Many that are doing well are offered for sale for a good reason. The firm remains profitable but the owner/operator:

- Died.
- Plans to retire.
- Has health issues.
- Wishes to do something else.
- Is getting divorced and his or her mate who is vital to the business will no longer be involved.

Clearly, many businesses are offered for sale because they are not doing well:
- They may never have achieved profitability.
- Many industries have changed and have faded out. Think of the stores that rented movies for home viewing.
- New competitors enter the neighborhood. Small local grocery stores and gas stations have been replaced by giants.
- The clientele has changed. For example, a toy store opened years ago in an area that had a high number of young couples and many children. All have aged and now the area is comprised mostly of retirees. Toys no longer sell in this neighborhood as they once did.

Major Advantages of Buying an Existing Business

- Financial history is available.
- Financing may be attained more easily.
- Assets are in place.
- The buyer has leverage.
- It is a turnkey operation.
- The seller can train the buyer.
- There is a higher probability of success.

Financial history: Tax records, Income Statements and Balance Sheets give a potential new owner a tremendous advantage in learning how and why a particular firm has performed over the years. An accountant or financial analyst can help quickly determine the value. Based on history and trends, a reasonable forecast for the next year or two should be achievable.

Financing: Generally, banks do not lend to new ventures. In fact, the same is true of the Small Business Administration which will lend to a small successful business needing funding for expansion. But both organizations are aware of the failure rate of startups.

Bank relationship: An existing company with a solid track record will likely have a positive relationship with a bank. The bank can see it has a positive cash flow and has successfully paid down loans. Thus, a seller can introduce a buyer to the bank and the buyer can usually assume the seller's role as customer, thereby gaining credit and financing.

Suppliers: They love to acquire the account of a startup. But they will insist payment of inventory on delivery until the new account has a reliable track record generally of more than one year. However, if an existing company is simply changing hands, the supplier will ask for proof the new owner has acceptable financial resources. If acceptable, the supplier will generally continue to extend existing credit terms.

Assets: The most valuable asset of most businesses is the staff, especially if trained and effective. (When new fast-food restaurants first open, for example, they often hire 20 percent more than needed because they know many new hires will not work out. By the end of the first month in operation, under-performing new hires are eliminated.)

Inventory: Sizes, flavors, colors, quantities, etc. are based on experience. Equipment and machinery are in place and operating.

Training: The buyer can be trained by the seller. This can be part of the deal. The buyer can take important notes regarding the strengths and weaknesses of employees, customers, suppliers, the landlord, banker, etc. The seller's experience is a great teacher.

"Tax records, Income Statements and Balance Sheets give a potential new owner a tremendous advantage in learning how and why a particular firm has performed over the years."

Buyer's Leverage

How many potential owner/operators want to own a laundromat?

How many prospective buyers would have the knowledge and experience to take over a pet shop?

How many people have the required license to buy and operate an electrical or plumbing business?

How many buyers have the required degrees and certificates to buy and operate a doctor's or dentist's practice?

It is extremely difficult to sell an ongoing concern. The seller must find someone willing to *buy it at this location, and at this price*. That is why sellers often hire a broker. Typically, a broker earns six percent to seven percent commission on the sale of a house. Because of the difficulty selling a firm, brokers often charge 10 percent. That is why the buyer has powerful bargaining power when it comes to negotiations.

Just as importantly, the buyer might have leverage on financing. Every seller would like to receive the total negotiated selling price at closing and walk away with the money. However, a buyer could state, "We have agreed on price. Now here are my terms: I will pay 25 percent down, and 25 percent a year over the next three years. I do not have the total funding, and banks are not likely to lend the balance. We can also agree to your right to assume the business should I default."

While this is not what the seller wants, he or she may be forced to accept because of the difficulty in selling. In this case, the seller must reluctantly provide most of the financing. **The best part is the revenue from operations will provide the cash over the next three years to pay for the firm's own acquisition!**

If the seller reluctantly does agree to accept payment over time, in all fairness, he or she should also receive interest on the unpaid balance from the buyer. The rate of interest becomes a negotiated issue.

After negotiations and the closing take place, the new owner gains an instant income stream because of buying a turnkey operation.

The probability of success is greatly enhanced because of the advantages of buying an *existing* company. Conversely, how many times have you passed a sign announcing the name and type of a *new* business about to open and you forecast that it would not be successful? Why is it that you have almost always been correct?

"It is extremely difficult to sell an ongoing concern. The seller must find someone willing to buy it at this location, and at this price."

Prepare a SWOT Analysis When Purchasing an Existing Business

Here is what an analysis might look like:

Strengths
- The location is in a high traffic area.
- All six current staff members appear pleasant and willing to help.
- The sales floor, storage area and office are kept orderly and clean.
- The establishment appears to benefit from a core of repeat customers.
- The fixed sign above the store is excellent and so is the neon sign in the window.
- The firm has paid bills on time and has earned a good credit relationship with suppliers. As the new owner you are likely to continue with favorable credit terms not available to a new business.
- This has been a growing and profitable business until 2020. The owner claims the downturn was totally due to COVID-19 and traffic began returning in 2021 and in 2022 slowly, but steadily.
- The present mix and depth of inventory is the result of trial and error. Slow moving items have been eliminated. What is now on hand is what the local market wants. Similarly, pricing is based on ongoing competitive analysis. The store has learned which items can stand a price increase and which cannot.

Weaknesses
- Only one of the employees has been with the firm for more than two years.
- Two of the five short-term staff members have an unprofessional appearance.
- The shopping center could use a facelift, but one is not currently in the landlord's plans.
- The site within the center does not have great visibility and is not near the high drawing retailers.

- The selling area is cramped, and storage would also benefit from an expansion. But the dental practice to the left is not likely to vacate nor the chiropractor on the right. The current space is locked in.

Opportunities
- Expand sales by using the name and knowledge of the core products to develop an offsite, online supplemental business.
- Buy the business and learn it. At the same time, engage a commercial real estate firm to scout a new and larger location with better visibility near a larger drawing retailer.
- Post COVID, if the business can return to its historical profitability, the cash flow can become the primary source of expansion funding.
- The present location could be the first among several towns. Your contacts have expressed a possible willingness to co-partner in opening satellite stores in near, but separate cities. Each could contain more than one location.

Threats
- The store is two months into the final year of a five-year lease. Previous years called for a three percent annual increase in rent. When the new lease is negotiated in about 10 months, it is likely the landlord will insist on annual rent increases at a much higher percentage.
- The area has slipped noticeably in the last five years. Two miles to the east, new houses, a new school and a new library are under development. Because many parcels of land are available, new retail centers could be on the town's drawing board.
- Historical profitability was built on store traffic. COVID may have changed everything. Former customers may have switched to Amazon and other online vendors.
- There is only one direct and not particularly formi-

dable competitor located in the southwest corner of the area. But a major chain perceiving the market is underserved could open a supercenter in an ideal location.

Seller's Expectation

Most sellers are first-time sellers. Having no experience in this task, they have a wild range of expectations as to what the firm is worth. Clearly, and reasonably first, the seller expects to be paid for the physical assets. (This is discussed in the next section.)

Additionally, sellers expect to be compensated for the years of hard work in building the business, generating the volume of revenue, and creating its reputation. Many refer to this as "goodwill."

A common expectation for the value of this goodwill is three years of sales. This is often the expectation from less sophisticated owners. Then the question arises: Which three years, the past or future?

The problem is sales are not the same as profit. Many startups follow this normal pattern: They sustain a loss in the first year, about break even in the second, and post a modest profit in the third.

Some businesses, due to no fault of their owners, sustained losses in the last few years because of COVID. Also consider businesses that simply are not profitable. Is it reasonable to expect the buyer to compensate the owner for his or her hard work if no profit is being generated?

The point is, the value of goodwill should be reflected in profitability. Accordingly, Net Profit Before Tax should be the focus of attention. This is discussed in the next section.

What the Purchase Price Usually Includes

Generally, the buyer is paying for two things:

1. The Current Market Value of the Physical Assets

Learning the original costs of the land, building, equipment, and inventory is extremely helpful. Then estimating their replacement costs is not usually difficult. But estimating their *current market value* is crucial. Both parties need to know, "What are the assets now worth given they generally have depreciated?"

The seller may seek to be paid the original cost so the original investment can be recouped. He may also argue, "If you had to buy them now, considering inflation, you would have to pay much more." True, but the buyer would argue, "If bought new, they would also have the latest enhancements and a longer useful life."

That is why the *current market value* of the equipment in place is usually the fairest price for both parties. It is less than both the original cost reflecting wear and tear, and less than the more expensive replacement cost. If there is a lot of equipment and machinery, an appraiser can be hired.

2. Projected Income Stream

Forecasting the projected income stream has always been a difficult task. It became more difficult because of two occurrences: COVID and rapid inflation.

> Supermarkets might not find estimating sales much of a chore since they have a long history and the virus caused little interruption of revenue.
>
> However, after COVID, firms totally reliant on customer visits did not know if the traffic would return. For example, many movie theaters closed per-

manently. Those that reopened experienced a slow return because visitors hesitated being in one room for a few hours with others, with or without masks.

Assuming a seller and potential buyer can arrive at a reasonable sales forecast, extrapolating expenses became more difficult due to steep inflation in 2022. Once again, supermarkets are in an enviable position because they can generally pass on higher costs to consumers. In turn, consumers may stop buying items they now believe are overpriced, but they still must buy food. Other sellers are not as fortunate. In some cases, higher expenses cannot fully be offset by raising prices. This puts a squeeze on bottom-line profit. Some businesses hereafter simply will not be as profitable as they once were.

These problems must be overcome. The potential buyer and the seller need a Projected Income Statement for at least three years and it may take the help of an accountant or financial analyst.

"Generally, the buyer is paying for two things: the current market value of the physical assets and the projected income stream."

Agreeing on a Selling Price

The following suggests a quick way of arriving at a selling price reasonable to both parties.

o From the previous section, assume Projected Income Statements have been prepared and the new owner will continue to charge the business the same $80,000 salary as the current owner has. After this expense and all other costs and expenses, assume the Net Profit Before Tax for the next three years is:

Year 1	Year 2	Year 3	Total
$ 45,000	$ 50,000	$55,000	$150,000

o Assume the current market value of the physical assets is $40,000 consisting mostly of the cost of inventory. (Assume the property is leased. Thus, the values of the land and the building are not issues.)

o The seller then justifies his asking price:

"Besides the nice salary you should be able to withdraw from the business, we have agreed to two things:

- First, the current market value of the physical assets is about $40,000.

- Second, over the next three years the store should clear about $150,000 in Net Profit Before Tax.

"A fair price should be $190,000. That is the estimated profit for the next three years totaling $150,000 + $40,000 for the *current market value* of the assets."

The potential buyer counters:
"If I can take $80,000 a year in salary, I will have earned it for working 50 or 60 or more hours per week and inheriting all the worries. If the business cannot afford it, I will have

89

to pay myself less.

> o "There is no guarantee the Net Profit numbers we are estimating will be realized. If they are, then I will be paying you three years of profit in advance. I will only be earning profit for myself beginning in year four and by then, the entire competitive environment will likely have changed.
>
> o "Here is my offer:
> - First, we can agree that the current market value of the physical assets is about $40,000.
>
> - Second, I will be willing to pay the Year 1 estimated profit which you get without having to do anything.

"My counteroffer is: $45,000 for the estimated Year 1 Net Profit Before Tax + $40,000 for the assets = $90,000."

The two deals are $100,000 apart. Splitting the difference is $50,000. A reasonable settlement becomes $140,000.

"Dollars do better if they are accompanied by sense."

Earl Rainey

Why Existing Businesses (and New Ones) Fail

Generally, there are three major reasons and sometimes a fourth reason for failure.

1. Under-Capitalized ("Capital" means investment)
2. Poor Planning
3. Poor Management
4. Bad Location

Under-Capitalized

A business that is under-capitalized implies it lacks sufficient cash, savings, and access to additional resources such as borrowing power or bringing in partners with more cash.

It would be rare for a new business to open with insufficient cash. That is not the problem. Almost always the firm has enough funding to launch the venture. It is the mindset of the owner that is the problem: "Even if we start slowly, once opened, the generated revenue should carry us through the second half of the year."

Because a new venture must start anew, acquiring each and every customer, even conservative sales forecasts tend to be overly optimistic.

When a new restaurant opens, even without the benefit of a marketing campaign, it attracts the curious, including those working for the competition. Initial weeks enjoy strong sales as customers come back for the second time. The honeymoon seems to fade after a few months as customers tend to return to their former pattern and former restaurants. It will then take marketing dollars to attract more new customers and to motivate the earlier ones to return.

Also, despite the best plans, new ventures discover problems requiring cash to fix. Examples:

-The front counter is too close to the entrance, forcing some customers to stand in the doorway with the door remaining open.

-The counter needs to be replaced by a new one 12 inches wider, 60 inches longer, and installed farther into the store.

-One microwave is not enough, causing orders to back up. A second one is needed and a third could be really helpful.

-Deliveries of crucial meat supplies are unreliable and coming from a great distance. Another refrigeration unit is needed to keep more inventory on hand and to prepare larger orders.

-Even unexpected problems requiring additional cash could cause havoc before opening. For example, a major corporation was building restaurants in malls. Two were being planned at opposite ends of a city. The first one opened with no problem, and it was constructed, barely within budget.

The second one, which was planned to be opened a month later, happened to be just outside the city limits. The town insisted an exhaust hood was required. A company representative spoke to town officials and explained that the restaurant does not fry anything and in six other locations in the East and Midwest, no hood was required. A town official replied, "That may be so, but similar restaurants in town have opened without a hood. Once up and running, they began frying food without a hood, creating a fire hazard. Therefore, we now require all restaurants to have a hood with a self-extinguishing fire feature.

At the time, the hood was $20,000 plus $2,000 installation. It was not expected, and it put the project over budget. But the company paid for the hood and installation. The hood delayed opening by two months during which the company had to pay rent with no revenue. That was $22,000! What would that "surprise" cost someone in today's dollars? What if this had been a small business owner?

Another example of unexpected costs: An existing business

is purchased and several months later THE critical piece of equipment – the computer system, a printing press, the pizza oven, the delivery truck – breaks down and is beyond repair. The new proprietor does not have the money or credit for a replacement.
Dry spells occur, both ordinary and extraordinary.

Ordinary slowdowns can be seasonal, economic, or weather-related.

Extraordinary might include international viruses as experienced by COVID spanning two-plus years, and local events such as spontaneous riots America has been experiencing with increased frequency. The police are accused of abusing a suspect. Store windows are smashed and looted, fires are set, etc. Cash from insurance claims does not always come quickly. Some claims are not covered.

In summary, the potential owner should plan for the worst. Assume that events beyond his control could limit the amount of cash he was planning to withdraw for himself and for his family to live on. It would be naïve to think the business will be a cash cow in its first year or two. Always assume an infusion of cash will be required for some unforeseeable reason after start-up or acquisition. Another reason to remember that Cash is King!

Poor Planning

It would be logical to agree with those who believe the number one reason why businesses fail is insufficient funding. Those who disagree say, "The primary reason for failure is poor planning, beginning with the need for cash and backing."

People who are considering a business they are familiar with have a critical advantage. They can likely see the road ahead. Those interested in a venture new to them absolutely need the assistance of a knowledgeable person who can offer advice as to where the industry is headed, and specifically, the firm under consideration.

Planning basics: Where is the business now? Where would you like to take it? How will you get there?

In addition to planning for capital needs, critical questions should be addressed. Here is a partial list:

1. How strong is the current or planned lineup of products and services?
2. Which stage of a normal life cycle are they in?
   - Introduction?
   - Growth?
   - Maturity/Saturation?
   - Decline?
- Where will growth likely come from?
- What are the possibilities for expansion?
- Who are the current direct competitors?
- Who are the indirect competitors?
- What are the competitors' strengths and weaknesses?
- If location is important, how would you rate the site and the terms of the lease?
- Employees
  - What are their concerns?
  - How will new hires be recruited and what will be the compensation package?
  - Who are the critical people and what if one or two decide to leave?

Poor Management

After acquiring an existing business, the new owner comes to the site with a headful of ideas. There is a temptation to make immediate changes, which disrupts current business practices. There are reasons things are done the current way. First learn why. Current methods are the result of alternatives that have been tried and replaced by the actions currently employed. Change can be disruptive.

The opposite may also be true. Listen to the employees. They may suggest immediate changes that are needed. For example, they may suggest replacing an antiquated cash register or point-of-sale system with a newer model. The owner did not want to make the investment since the intention was to sell the business, but an upgrade is badly needed because of the amount of times the current system crashes.

Managing is "getting things done through people." Successful managers share many traits:
- They are aware the most important assets of the company are the employees.
- They hire local college students majoring in management and marketing for part time work.
- They recognize employees:
    - Are working for the firm to maximize their own income
    - Generally welcome overtime if they will be paid at time-and-a-half
    - Love to hear two words: "bonus" and "promotion"
- They praise in public and criticize in private. In doing so, they will compliment an employee in front of fellow staff members and customers. When necessary, they privately criticize an employee's negative behavior.
- When it is necessary to reprimand a staff member, they use a "sandwich" approach. They begin with a compliment: "We know how valuable you are to us." They address the issue: "But lately you seem to get annoyed with customers too easily. That lady tossed the item on the counter and then walked out." Having made the point, they close the session on a positive note: "You are generally very patient with customers even after spending a lot of time with them. They usually leave the store with a purchase and walk away happy."
- Managers take time to see the business from a customer's viewpoint:

- How does the location appear from the parking lot? Welcoming or need of a face lift?
- Are the signs on the building and in the display window easy to read?
- How is the aroma when you enter the building?
- Is the background music too loud and distracting?
- Are customers greeted professionally, or too casually, such as, "How are ya?" or "Can I help ya?"
- Are there many gaps in missing inventory? Are the aisles neat and passable?
- Are the restrooms clean and orderly? Are they cleaned regularly? Remember: "Cleanliness is next to godliness."

Bad Location

There is an old saying regarding the three critical things in real estate: Location, location, location.

First, determine if the venture is more destination or parasitic.

A specialist such as a heart doctor can be located almost anywhere since a referred patient will track down the office. The business is destination oriented.

But a small business specializing in shoes or upscale clothing will benefit by parasitically drawing from the traffic generated by the shopping center's major anchor – typically a supermarket or department store.

Among the mistakes small business owners make is selecting a site because of its affordable rent. There is a reason the rent may appear to be affordable or even a bargain. Unsuccessful owners have said, "I picked this spot because better locations I considered would have consumed any money for marketing." A small business in a great retail location often spends little or nothing on marketing because it is not needed.

People who shop at a supermarket can park and venture a few doors away and stop by a clothing store even if it was an unplanned visit. They spot a bargain and can justify making a purchase by thinking, "I could always use this."

The name of the game is not to minimize rent. Usually, the competitor with the lowest rent does not survive. An owner should be willing and able to afford to pay the landlord for a spot in a center drawing many carloads of customers daily.

Where and how people are shopping, though, has changed drastically. One newspaper article reports that on average, one mall per day – about 365 per year – is closing in the country. And, of course, one of the reasons is that an increasing number of consumers are buying online.

Investing in a Franchise

Becoming a franchise owner – a franchisee – is generally less risky than buying many existing businesses. There are many advantages to operating under the wings of a franchisor who has a proven business model and a record of success. But there are also many disadvantages. Evaluate a franchise thoroughly before deciding if this is the route you want to take. Study the pluses and minuses:

Pluses:

+ The probability of success is significantly higher than starting a new business or purchasing an existing one.

+ There is instant brand and product recognition accompanied by goodwill.

+ Franchisor generally has both company-owned and franchised units. From both, over the years lessons have been learned as to the keys of success. Similarly, failures have been studied along with solutions.

+ Franchisor investigates the applicant's financial qualifications. If judged insufficient, the applicant is denied. This tends to lower the possibility of a unit failing because of under-capitalization.

+ Franchisor provides valuable training in a classroom and in an operating unit. Thereafter, if the applicant does not pass a qualifying test, the applicant is denied. This tends to lessen the likelihood a unit will fail due to poor management.

+ If it is a retail location, the franchisor must approve the desired location and at times will help with leasing information and negotiations. This tends to prevent a unit failing because of a poor location.

+ If the applicant and the site are approved, the franchisee is granted exclusivity within an area such as five square miles. Some companies will grant a very strong financial applicant such as a large corporation seeking diversification the designation "Master Franchisee." The master is given the exclusive right to an entire state. Then prepares a rollout plan for development. It could call for and commit to five new locations annually, for the next five years. The franchisee benefits since he gains a legal monopoly for expansion with the concept. The franchisor benefits since the core business will be brought to an entire state and become a future revenue stream with no cost.

+ Franchisor continuously invests in research, then passes on its findings and recommendations. Topics include legislation, competition analysis, new product development, training, quality control, sanitation, testing new equipment, and new technology.

+ Franchisor typically has a Marketing Fund. It develops advertising and sales promotion campaign shared by company owned and franchised units at a cost lower than a business owner can experience alone.

+ Franchisor typically has a Purchasing Cooperative that buys in huge quantities, thereby gaining quantity discounts. Through the Cooperative, all units can obtain raw materials, packaging, supplies, equipment, signage and more.

+ There is strength in numbers. Often a franchisee Advisory Association has been formed. Suggestions, concerns and complaints are shared. Then with a unified voice they can be passed on to the franchisor.

Minuses:

- Initially, this is often the most expensive way to get into a business since all the benefits a franchisor provides come at a price.

- To join the club there is a hefty initial Franchise Fee.

- There is a Continuing Royalty ranging from three percent to seven percent of a franchisee's revenue that must be paid monthly to the franchisor. This obligation to share a portion of revenue must be paid like any other monthly expense regardless of whether the franchisee's business is profitable.

- The Marketing Fund is an additional charge to each franchisee.

- Franchisor pins a map when moving into a state or large area. Then cherry picking occurs: Where a cluster of units can be located and monitored by an area manager, the franchisor develops company owned and operated stores. Then outlining areas are made available to potential franchisees.

- Loss of independence: A McDonald's franchisee cannot independently decide to offer hot dogs. The franchisor strives for consistency and rules with an iron hand. Regional inspectors visit units to ensure policies and procedures are being followed. Violators are compelled to make changes. If they do not, their franchise rights can be terminated.

- The franchise agreement is for a certain number of years requiring renewal by both parties. Years ago, it was common for the term to be 20 years. Towards expiration, old establishments tended to lose business to new competition and the unit tended to be "dated" or clearly run-down. Owners could not afford the necessary improvements, forcing the franchisor to allow the term to expire and refuse to renew. More recently, the common term has been reduced to 10 years, allowing the franchisor more control over continuing operations.

- From the above minuses, it is not surprising lawsuits are quite common.

About the Author

In Anthony Zaffuto's nearly 60 years in business and academia, he was on teams that purchased and managed companies and taught others how to do it. He understands what it takes to succeed.

His experience is the basis for offering practical advice to anyone who is thinking of starting or buying a business, including a franchise.

Anthony earned bachelor's and master's degrees in Economics and Finance before beginning his career with three Fortune 500 companies. He began as a Financial Analyst with the Columbia Gas System in Manhattan. He then joined The Singer Company holding mid management positions in finance, management, and market research.

Thereafter he worked for R.J. Reynolds for 16 years when the primarily tobacco company was seeking growth through diversification. He was the Financial Manager of several food brands, including College Inn Chicken and Beef Products, Patio Mexican Food, Chun King Oriental Food, My-T-Fine Puddings and Pies, Vermont Maid Syrup, Brer Rabbit Syrup and Molasses, and Davis Baking Powder. He then was part of the team that bought the Burmah Oil Company. At the time it was among America's largest acquisitions. Research and acquisition of Nabisco, Del Monte, and Kentucky Fried Chicken followed.

He rose to Director of New Businesses and Vice President of two R.J. Reynolds Nabisco subsidiaries for which he prepared business plans for national expansion. For the first one, he led the acquisition of Skolniks Bagel Bakery Restaurants and then built five new locations in very upscale malls. Then for Reynolds he became the franchisee of

Fresher Cooker Restaurants. Thereafter, he became Director of Strategic Planning for Hawaiian Punch, Canada Dry and Sunkist.

He also has served as a consultant, lecturer, and university professor.

As a consultant, Anthony completed assignments for Martin Marietta/General Electric, Sonny's BBQ, Palmer Chiropractic College and several small firms in strategic planning, management, marketing, and finance.

He has been a speaker to such groups as the American Management Association, NationsBank, chambers of commerce and others. In addition, he was a guest discussing entrepreneurship on two public television shows.

During a period of 20 years, he taught 30 college business subjects in Finance, Economics, Marketing, Management, and Entrepreneurship at The University of Central Florida, Embry-Riddle Aeronautical University, Keiser University, Bethune-Cookman University, and Daytona Beach State College. Additionally, he earned an Outstanding Educator Award for his contribution to the online Business Program at the University of Florida through excellence in teaching and academic guidance.

Successful Entrepreneurs & Leaders

We Write & Publish Your Book

Business Success Books · Biographies

Promote Your Business with Your Book
- Unique, Affordable Marketing.
- Reach New Customers & Clients.
- Stand Out from Your Competition.
- Be Recognized as an Authority in Your Industry.
- Being a Published Author Adds to Your Credibility.
- Earn Royalties on Book Sales.

Retired or Semi-Retired?
- We Write the Story of Your Success and Lessons Learned.
- Share Your Business Knowledge from Decades of Experience.
- Teach. Inspire. Motivate.
- Preserve the Legacy. Share the Memories.

For **Entrepreneurs, CEOs,
Business Owners, Leaders, Speakers**,
and **Executives** and **Professionals** in
Virtually Any Industry or Profession.

BizSuccessBooks.com
LegaciesandMemories.com

Award-Winning Writing

LegaciesandMemories.com

PURCHASE ONLINE

- Amazon.com
- BarnesandNoble.com
- Bookshop.org
- Other retailers

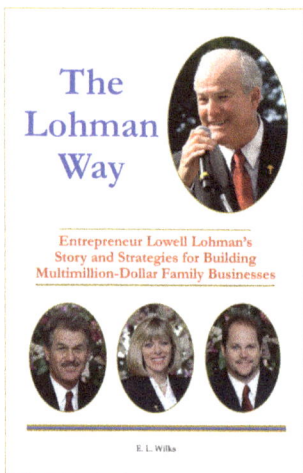

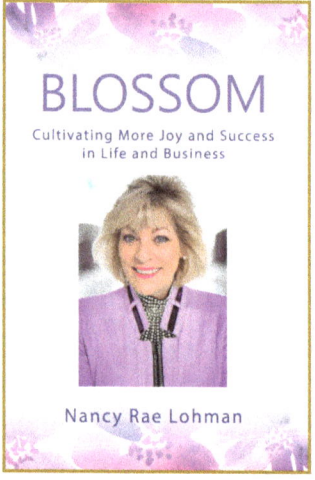

BizSuccessBooks.com · LegaciesandMemories.com
(888) 862-2754

We Write The Book

For Your Family or Business

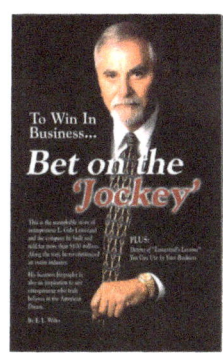

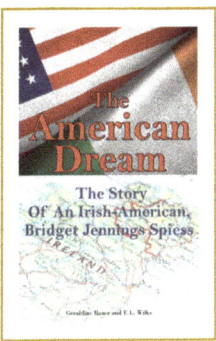

Corporate History

Publisher of Award-Winning Books
Purchase Online

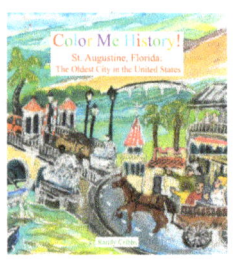
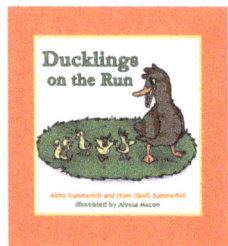
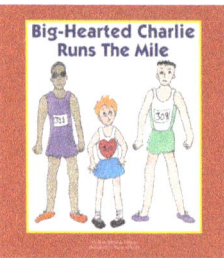
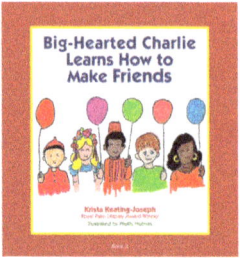
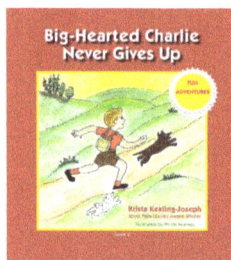
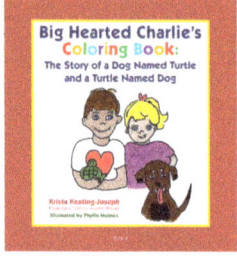

LegaciesandMemoriesPublishing.com

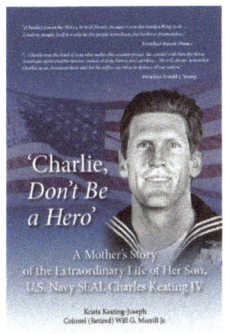
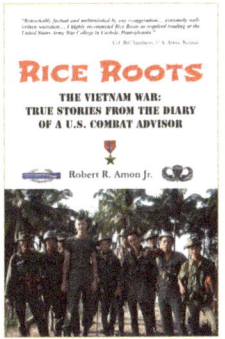

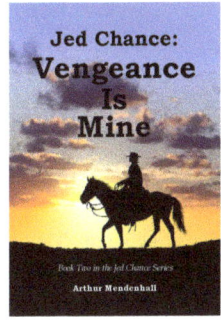

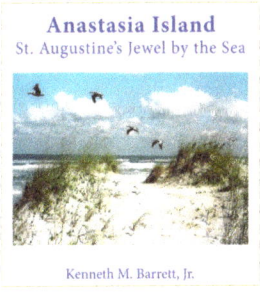
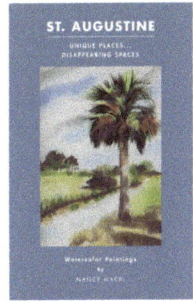

LegaciesandMemoriesPublishing.com

www.ingramcontent.com/pod-product-compliance
Lightning Source LLC
Chambersburg PA
CBHW061146170426
43209CB00011B/1573